EXPECTING
GOD TO SPEAK
TO YOU!

EXPECTING GOD TO SPEAK TO YOU!

Tracy Williamson

New Wine Press

New Wine Ministries
PO Box 17
Chichester
West Sussex
United Kingdom
PO20 6YB

ISBN 1-903725-41-0

Typeset by CRB Associates, Reepham, Norfolk
Cover design by CCD, www.ccdgroup.co.uk
Printed in the United States of America

For information about Tracy Williamson or Marilyn Baker Ministries, please write to:

Marilyn Baker Ministries
PO Box 393
Tonbridge
Kent
TN9 9AY

or visit the web site:

www.marilynbakerministries.org

CONTENTS

Dedication   9

Acknowledgements   11

Foreword   13

Introduction   15

Chapter 1   Tuning in to God's voice   21

Chapter 2   Seeking for hidden treasure   33

Chapter 3   The God of creation and everyday life 51

Chapter 4   Hearing God through His children   69

Conclusion   85

About the author   87

DEDICATION

I would like to dedicate this book to my lovely friend Penny Cooze who died in May 2004 after a courageous fight against cancer. Despite a traumatic childhood and the struggles of blindness and illness, Penny was a true example of what it means to be open to the loving voice of God. You taught me so much, Penny.

"Now we see but a poor reflection as in a mirror; then we shall see face to face. Now I know in part; then I shall know fully, even as I am fully known."

(1 CORINTHIANS 13:12)

ACKNOWLEDGEMENTS

Grateful thanks to my many friends and faithful prayer supporters who have stood in love and prayer with me throughout the writing of this book.

Thanks to Lilian and Jennie, and other friends for being such an inspiration in listening to God and who have lovingly borne with me being distracted for so long!

Thanks to Marilyn for being a wonderful friend and ministry partner. For sacrificing time together so I could write, and for speaking God's words to me on so many occasions.

To Loyola Hall where I went on retreat as I started writing this book and through it experienced the powerful, healing presence of God.

To Patrick, whose prophetic word in January 2004 gave me the push to start writing again.

Most of all to the Lord Jesus without whose incredible love, this book could never have been written.

FOREWORD

Until I first met Tracy, about fifteen years ago, I had no idea just how difficult life can be for a person who is deaf – particularly when their sight is not good enough for sign language or lip reading. Tracy has become a very close friend yet I can't just pick up the phone when I want to talk to her and when we are together I have to write down every word I want to say in the notebook she calls "Gossip". She probably often feels lonely when conversations go on around her but she can't join in and by the time a joke is written down it does not seem nearly so funny.

Yet, in spite of the fact that Tracy cannot hear what people say she has a far greater capacity to hear God than anyone else I have ever met. All the sounds that distract the rest of us are missing for her and, because God's voice is the only one she can hear, His words are extremely distinct. I have heard people pouring out all their problems to Tracy at great length, quite unaware that she cannot hear a word they are saying. Inwardly she is listening to God so that He can tell her what *His* answer is for this person's problem. When Tracy gently tells them what He has been saying they are often amazed at how much healing and comfort they receive.

Tracy believes that we could all hear God's voice speaking just as clearly as she can, if only we would train ourselves to listen. This book is the fruit of many years of practising this skill and teaching others to listen too. I have had the fun of helping her run workshops on this subject a number of times. So often people say, "But I'm not the kind of person who hears God," but by the end of the day they are amazed at what they have heard Him say! I remember one lady who felt just like that and she became increasingly irritated as other people described what God had said through the flowers and pictures Tracy had provided, or the view from the open window. She was even more irritated because her seat was just behind the overhead projector, so she could not see Tracy's face as she talked. She had just decided to complain about this when she felt God say that her new hobby was becoming so absorbing and all-important that it was preventing her from seeing *His* face, just like the overhead projector!

Life becomes an adventure when you are open for God to speak to you at any time, through all the ordinary little things you see, hear and touch each day. I am sure that this book will draw many people into a far closer relationship with God than they have ever enjoyed before.

Jennifer Rees Larcombe

Introduction

The Heart and Power of Relationship with God

Listening is a matter of love and honour. When you choose to listen to someone, to put aside your own activities or opinions in order to take in theirs, you are saying to that person, "I respect you enough to listen to you. I believe you've got something important to say." This is the message we give God when we choose to listen to Him. We are telling Him we love and respect Him and think He has something important to say. Listening is an act of worship and heart love. Conversely, when we don't make time to listen to God, or anyone for that matter, we are effectively saying to them: "What you say is not as important as other things in my life. I don't believe you've got anything worthwhile to say to me. I don't respect or love you enough to find out what is on your heart."

You may think, that's crazy, I could never think that about God, but our actions speak louder than our words.

90% of our time is spent in activity *for* God rather than time *with* God and many do not even realise that God is longing to speak to them. Why is this?

Busyness, ignorance, lack of teaching, fear, all can play their part in keeping us from listening to God. Many of us also feel a deep sense of worthlessness and can't really believe that God will want to speak to *me*, but that very attitude, if we insist on holding it long term, speaks of the fact that we believe more in the authenticity of negative experiences or regrets than in God's words – that He sees us as clean and pure; as beloved as His son Jesus.

The Start of My Journey

I became a Christian at the end of my first year of college. I was eighteen and had never been exposed to Christianity before. Going to college to train to be a teacher and the subsequent realization that I was too deaf to do it (added to the fact that I didn't have the right temperament), brought to the surface deep and painful emotions. There were many overwhelming struggles from my childhood that I had buried over the years, not knowing how to deal with them. Suddenly confronted with these "spectres", I became suicidally depressed.

It was in the midst of this crisis that Ruth, another student, gave me my first experience of the fact that people can hear God. One day she invited me into her room and told me that she had been praying that week and God had brought me to her mind. He said to her, "Tracy needs to know Me as a Father." She said, "Do you understand what I am talking about?"

To say that I was staggered was an understatement. God, who didn't even exist as far as I was concerned, was telling someone my name, asking them to pray for me and telling them about one of the most vulnerable areas in my life. No, I did not understand, but suddenly I wanted to.

The ensuing conversation about the reality and love of God was the beginning of a new road for me, one that I have been travelling on ever since. I opened my heart to God about six weeks later and began to discover what being a Christian meant.

The problem was, I had lived on the surface of my life for so long that I instinctively began to do the same in my new Christian life. I went to church with the other students, read my Bible, prayed, sang ... and felt nothing. There was still so much pain inside that I did what I had always done, buried it and just carried on living, albeit, now in a Christian way.

One day everything blew up. A negative remark from another student acted as the fuse and suddenly I was consumed with the strongest feelings of grief and anger that I had ever experienced. Bizarrely, the force of the anger was God-directed. I felt betrayed by Him – that I had put my whole trust in Him to change and heal me, but nothing had happened. Now there was nothing else I could do but go. I could not stay any longer surrounded by the very people that had helped me to hope again. If I couldn't stay with them, then neither could I remain a student. I had to leave.

Many hours and miles later I stumbled into a bus shelter and sat down exhausted. It was pouring with rain and I was soaked, but still full of turmoil. I had no idea what I was

going to do. I had no money, clothes or food. I had just run
with what I had with me – textbooks! One thing I was sure
of though: I was never going back.

Suddenly, I heard a voice. It came out of the darkness
and spoke so clearly that I could hear every word.

"Tracy, I love you and want to be a Father to you."

Shocked, I leapt to my feet, convinced someone else was
there, but the bus shelter was deserted. It was a lonely
country road in the middle of a storm. There was no one
there but me – and God. It was God who had just spoken
to me, even in the midst of my turmoil and angry thoughts.

For the next hour I sat and talked with God. I forgot the
"Christian jargon" I'd already picked up. I just told Him
how hurt, angry and confused I was feeling.

And He talked back to me.

He told me that He loved me and always would love me;
that nothing could ever make Him turn His back on me,
even if I left Him. He told me that He truly wanted to be a
Father to me and for me to be a "real" child – to be able to
come to Him like a child comes to her parents, sharing both
the good and bad things of her life, trusting in their care,
help and encouragement. He said that the whole point of
Jesus dying was to bring me into this real, trusting relationship with Him as my Daddy. He promised that as I opened
up to Him, He would pour His healing and freedom into
my life and bring about the change I longed for.

How Did God Tell Me This?

When God first spoke to me that momentous evening, it
seemed almost like an audible voice.

This next part was different. It was as if my mind was being directed along lines that were contrary to my own thoughts and feelings. Truths from His Word were dropping into my consciousness along with words and phrases that came so simply into my mind it was almost as if I was thinking my own thoughts.

Yet, I knew this wasn't me. The impressions were bringing with them a deep sense of peace and hope that my own thoughts simply had never had. Even when I'd previously tried positive thinking techniques, my thoughts had always been in turmoil underneath. Now I could sense a stillness coming over me. I was able to let go of my anger and come to a place of willingness to go back and start again.

WE CAN ALL HEAR HIM

That night I was in a place of weakness and anger, but God still spoke to me. God speaks because we are His children and He loves us. Anyone who has put their trust in Jesus can hear God. Jesus said,

> *"My sheep listen to my voice. I know them and they follow me."*
> (JOHN 10:27)

In our journey to discover how to listen to God, we can try certain techniques, which can be very beneficial. People have said many times after attending a "Listening to God" workshop, "I never realised that God would speak personally to me through such everyday things" or "I thought I'd never heard God – that I didn't match up as a Christian –

but now I realise that I'd been hearing Him all along; I'd just not listened!"

That is why this book has come about.

If you are one of the many who have a longing to hear God, but don't quite know how, then this book is for you. Each chapter will be sharing different aspects of listening with lots of stories and practical suggestions, but far more than that it is a book of love and passion. This love I have sensed in Father God's heart for each one of us His precious children, to draw near to Him in meaningful relationship, to share our lives with Him and to hear His transforming words of love and power.

CHAPTER 1

TUNING IN TO GOD'S VOICE

MAKE OUR MINDS BLANK?

In a workshop I once led on listening to God, someone asserted, "I've got to make my mind as blank as blank. I've got to erase every bit of 'me thought' and then I will be able to hear God."

The good news is that this is almost the opposite of the truth!

While it is true that we do need to open our minds up to God and come into a place of inner stillness and trust before Him, as He says in Psalm 46:10, *"Be still and know that I am God"*, this in no way means that we have to make our minds blank or go into any kind of "detached from self" experience. In fact, it is impossible to make our minds blank in a good way and to try to do this opens us up to attack from the devil rather than inspiration from God! The devil's main battleground is our minds and he will take every opportunity to infiltrate and take control. Some occult practices deliberately advocate and facilitate this. They talk about clearing our minds of all intrusive thoughts, going into trance-like states and reaching a higher level of consciousness into which God can make His presence known. The mention of God gives a sense of it all being OK, but remember, the devil is very subtle. The word "occult" means "hidden" and that is exactly what it is; it hides behind the truth of God, appearing to be good and Christian, but in reality distorting and twisting it.

Jesus was very specific about the devil's strategies. He said,

> *"He was a murderer from the beginning, not holding to the truth, for there is no truth in him. When he lies he speaks his native language for he is a liar and the father of lies ... He who belongs to God hears what God says."*
>
> (JOHN 8:44, 47)

Jesus clearly states the criteria for hearing God. No, it's not to do with the reaching of higher states of being or contacting God once our minds have been made as clear as glass. Neither is it to do with any form of denial or abasement of who we are. These are all the ways of the liar and murderer Satan. The criteria, quite simply, is that *we belong to God*!

BELONGING TO GOD

But, I hear you say, if it really is as simple as that, why is there so much division in the church? Why do so many Christians say they have never heard God speaking to them? While others who declare they do hear Him, say things in His name that bring devastation?

Jesus was telling us the starting point for our ability to hear God and follow Him. We can expect to hear Him because we belong to Him. Hearing Him is a learning process for all of us and we will not be 100% good at it until we meet Him face to face! But the starting point is that we come to God who is someone who has chosen us to be His children and loves us in the way that only the most perfect Father ever could. We have changed from having no real connection with anybody because of the Fall, to having the most incredible and eternal connection with the Creator of the universe! This is what Jesus calls *belonging*. Peter also expresses this:

> *"But you are a chosen people, a royal priesthood, a holy nation, a people belonging to God that you may declare the praises of him who called you out of darkness into his wonderful light. Once you were not a people, but now you are the people of God; once you had not received mercy, but now you have received mercy."*
>
> (1 PETER 2:9–10)

The moment we put our trust in Jesus, we are transferred into the new position of belonging to God and nothing can ever snatch us away from Him. The reason we do not have to reach a higher level of consciousness is because we already have it! At that precise moment of joining with God He gives us two precious gifts:

> " 'No eye has seen,
>   no ear has heard,
>   no mind has conceived
>   what God has prepared for those who love Him' –
>
> but God has revealed it to us by his Spirit. The Spirit searches all things, even the deep things of God. For who among men knows the thoughts of a man except the man's spirit within Him? In the same way, no-one knows the thoughts of God except the Spirit of God. We have not received the spirit of the world but the Spirit who is from God, that we may understand what God has freely given us."
>
> (1 CORINTHIANS 2:9–12)

> " 'For who has known the mind of the Lord
>   that he may instruct him?'
>
> But we have the mind of Christ."
>
> (1 CORINTHIANS 2:16)

WE HAVE THE MIND OF CHRIST

When God spoke to me that night in the bus shelter He was operating through these two gifts: His Holy Spirit and the mind of Christ. We receive the mind of Christ at salvation.

It is the ability to tune into the very thoughts of God. Our own spirits have come alive and can now connect with God's Spirit whom Jesus describes as our comforter, counsellor and convictor, amongst other things (see John 14, 15 and 16). We all have a unique way of thinking and understanding, and the Holy Spirit, the only one who knows the thoughts of God, also knows each one of us. So He takes the thoughts of God (the mind of Christ) and communicates them to us into our own minds and hearts.

How Will This Happen?

This will happen in different ways with different people. Some may get a strong feeling of unease or peace, or a sensation that they should do or say a certain thing. Others may get a visual impression or dream. Some may get a verse or Bible passage coming to mind. Some may find certain words and phrases, or sudden knowledge about someone or a situation, dropping into their consciousness. Some may find that a sermon that has been preached, a song sung, words of advice from a friend etc., can suddenly take on a deep sense of significance. Others may find that same sense of significance suddenly "hitting" them as they do everyday tasks or deliberately meditate on the Bible, creation, or ordinary things around them. We will be looking at all these areas in greater depth in the coming chapters. The key is that we are coming to Someone wonderful who loves us and who wants to communicate with us and knows how to do it.

BETTER THAN THE BEST

Jesus said:

> *"I no longer call you servants, because a servant does not know his master's business. Instead, I have called you friends, for everything that I learned from my Father I have made known to you."*
>
> (JOHN 15:15)

The New Testament brings alive the concepts of both the friendship and the Fatherhood of God, and communication is central to both. Whatever good things we experience in both those relational areas with others, should be all the better in our relationship with God. As I found in that bus shelter experience, I had listened to people before and I had tried to think positively, but to no avail. However, when God spoke of His Father-love to me that night, a powerful peace came with the words that brought me into a place of heart stillness and hope.

As it says in Hebrews 4:12,

> *"For the word of God is living and active. Sharper than any double-edged sword, it penetrates even to dividing soul and spirit, joints and marrow; it judges the thoughts and attitudes of the heart."*

Hearing God's voice is better than hearing any other voice, because His very words are full of creative, life-changing power. The Bible is not just a collection of words that were spoken thousands of years ago – it is full of the present-day power of God, able to reach into our lives and situations in a way that nothing else can. "The Word of God" also refers to the person of Jesus, the "living word" and to every Spirit-inspired word that comes from God.

SO IF WE DON'T HAVE TO MAKE OUR MINDS BLANK, WHAT DO WE DO?

Firstly there is no simple answer because listening to God can never be method alone, but the heart's response to love!

God will want to speak to you at different times for different reasons and therefore the way you prepare yourself to hear will also take different forms. Here are some common ways in which God wants to speak to you:

▶ *He may quite simply want to suddenly catch your attention, a bit like a friend or family member calling you when you are busy. You stop what you are doing and go to see what they want (hopefully!).*

With a friend doing this, you physically hear them call. With God it is different. We don't physically hear Him, at least not very often. What does happen is that we get a sudden awareness in our hearts; something seems important and you can't stop thinking about God, or a person, or an activity, or a specific verse. This is when you can do the equivalent of going to see what your friend wants. You can say to the Lord, "Lord, are you trying to speak to me?" and then listen to see if further revelation comes to you. The other day, for example, I was with a friend. We'd had lunch in a café and then taken the dog for a walk in the fields nearby. As we returned we passed the café and saw the lady who had served us at the till having a cigarette outside. My friend chatted to her for a few minutes. I didn't, because of the difficulty of hearing her. But suddenly, as we moved away, I found myself thinking about her and the fact that she had been outside. Eventually I said to the Lord, "Are you trying to speak to me?" I became aware of His deep love for her and His promise that even if people had "put her outside" and rejected her, He never would. If she trusted in Him she would find a love that would never leave her. We went back to the café and I told her this. She was so open and thrilled to think that God had spoken to us for her.

You may think, I will never know if it is God speaking to me. I will probably miss those sudden awarenesses!

One thing that can be helpful is to quite simply tell the Lord at the beginning of each day that you want to be close to Him that day, and then be open to the Holy Spirit's enabling and leading. Simply get on with whatever you have to do that day, trusting that if God wants to speak to you He will know how to get your attention. That is His responsibility. Ours is to listen and respond.

▶ *He may want to draw close to you and put His thoughts in your heart to edify, comfort or challenge you or to give you a new awareness of what He is like or His purposes and heart for a given time.*

This will involve a different kind of listening process. Here, you are deliberately asking and expecting God to be close and to speak to you. You are consciously making time for Him, whether that is a few moments, half an hour, or a day. This is *not* a process of making your mind blank, but it *is* a process of stopping other activities so that you can focus on God; then, within that focusing, giving Him the time and space to communicate with you as well as you expressing your prayers to Him.

For example, on one occasion, Marilyn and I were in a prayer meeting with a committee who had organised the concert we were about to do. It is tempting in prayer meetings like this to simply tell God to anoint and bless the event etc. But sometimes God wants to tell us something too! The same thing applies with anything we want God to bless and help us with. We had felt a sense of heaviness, so I quietly asked the Lord if there was anything He wanted to say. I found my attention being drawn to the carpet which had a thick pile. I noticed a streak in it where the pile had been brushed the wrong way. This seemed significant. As I continued to pray silently, God showed me that the streak in the carpet symbolised divisions and negative gossip going on in this church. He said that the hallmark of Christians is meant to be unity and love, but this divisiveness was becoming the hallmark and showing up to outsiders like the streak in the carpet. That was the word! But I still needed to hear from Him as to what He wanted me to do with it. Sometimes He wants us to share what He gives us, other times just to acknowledge it, and at other times to intercede in a specific way because of it. As I continued to listen, I knew that He wanted me to share it in a loving way. I did and at the end several repented including some of the leaders.

▶ *We can ask Him to speak to us through a particular thing, for example, the Bible.*

Sometimes, as we read the Bible, it may be that a sudden passage catches our attention, almost as if it has been highlighted. This is an example of the first way of hearing Him. This is vital but must never replace regular reading and study. As we read we can say to Him, "Lord what does this show me about You? What does it show me about Your ways? What does it show me about myself? Is there any way I need to change my heart picture of You or myself to be in line with what You are showing me here?" And then listen to what comes to your heart from that passage. In a similar way you can choose to deliberately focus on creation or some everyday thing around you and ask God to speak to you through it.

There was one occasion when we had just acquired our cat, Zoë. She was very young and frightened in her new surroundings. I was trying to reach her under the dining table to give her a cuddle, but she just kept jumping from one chair seat to another. I felt frustrated because I only wanted to love her. I wondered if the Lord wanted to teach me something through this and so asked Him to speak to me. As I watched Zoë wriggling away from me, He showed me that was often what I did with Him. All He wanted to do was to love me, but often I would do anything but come into His presence. I realised this was true and unknowingly, I was transferring past negative experiences onto God, making me draw back from Him. Needless to say this challenged and encouraged me to come to Him much more trustingly.

In this chapter I have shared some of the basics of tuning in to the voice of God. I will develop these more fully throughout the rest of the book and will give you creative ideas to try out. Remember, this is a journey of discovery and the most exciting and loving Person of all is travelling it with you!

CHAPTER 2

SEEKING FOR HIDDEN TREASURE

" ... if you accept my word ... and if you look for it
as for silver, and search for it as for hidden treasure,
then you will understand the fear of the LORD and
find the knowledge of God."
(PROVERBS 2:1–5 paraphrased)

As a child I had a friend called Neil. We lived near wood-
lands and often pretended that we were searching for buried
treasure. We had to outwit the enemy and the moment of

discovery was exhilarating! Such was the wonder of child-hood make-believe, transforming an old cache of stones into exotic treasure!

THE BIBLE IS BURIED TREASURE

One of the first Christian books I read was *Prayer: Key to Revival* by Paul Yonggi Cho. He describes the Bible like this: "When I pick up the most precious material possession I own, the Bible ..."[1] To Yonggi Cho that one item was priceless beyond anything. What gave it that special value to him and what does God want it to be for us?

Listen to this powerful description of God's word:

> *"For the word of God is living and active. Sharper than any double-edged sword, it penetrates even to dividing soul and spirit, joints and marrow, it judges the thoughts and attitudes of the heart."*
>
> (HEBREWS 4:12)

When I think about this sharp, penetrating weapon, I long to learn how to wield it. In the film, *The Lord of the Rings*, it is awesome when the king's broken sword is restored and, in the hands of its rightful owner, defeats the enemy. God's Word is described as a sword because it is powerful! So much can be transformed in our lives and in our world as we, the rightful owners, use it.

In real swordplay you don't just wave the sword around! You watch for a weak spot in your opponent's defence and immediately cut in with a clean thrust. Sometimes we can wave all sorts of conflicting verses around as we pray, but we must ask God to reveal His purposes through His Word and then with our faith imagination declare and pronounce it into being.

Recently, I was walking through the beautiful Welsh hills. I asked the Lord for insight about Wales. The passage where Jesus weeps for Jerusalem came to mind and I sensed His grief at the spiritual barrenness. Then another passage about the valleys being raised, the mountains levelled, and the glory of the Lord revealed (Isaiah 40:4–5). In my imagination, I saw the mountains of occult worship smashed down and the valleys of barrenness and suffering filling up with God's mercy and revival fire. I took that verse and "wielded" it as a sword. In other words, I didn't *ask* for it to happen, I *declared* to Satan and to everything that was within those mountains and valleys, that this verse *would* come to pass.

Once Marilyn and I counselled someone who couldn't forgive himself. We explained the forgiveness of God which only resulted in more despair. But then we declared some of Psalm 103: *"As far as the east is from the west, so far has he removed our transgressions from us ... "* (verse 12). Suddenly there was a bang! The man who had previously been huddled in defeat was on his feet, a huge smile on his face. The power of God's Word had broken through his condemnation and set him free.

BOREDOM WITH THE BIBLE?

Yet, while we know it is vital, the reality is often that we are bored with the Bible! We pick it up with a sigh! We think, "Oh I've read that, I'm familiar with it ... "

In my book *The Voice of the Father* I tell how, one night when I was a child, I discovered a tiny Bible. I tried to read it, but the language was too archaic. Disillusioned, I returned it to the shelf. Years later, God brought that memory to mind. I realised, as I prayed, that it had given me a deep sense of cynicism towards the Bible. Disparaging comments by "important" people, only confirmed what I thought was true. So now, even though I was a Christian who wanted more than anything to discover what God was like, my spirit was still deadened by this message: the Bible is dull, boring and irrelevant.[2]

The fact is, that while our spirits have been made new, we can still be "controlled" by the old ways of thinking. These act as an invisible fence, restraining us whenever we try to move forward with God. The more we recognise what those areas of negativity are, and give them to God, the more we will receive all that God wants for us. As it says in Romans,

> *"Do not conform any longer to the pattern of this world, but be transformed by the renewing of your mind. Then you will be able to test and approve what God's will is – his good pleasing and perfect will."*
>
> (ROMANS 12:2)

Not conforming is a choice *I* make! I see an area of my life where I am just going along with everyone else; I realise it isn't good; I talk and listen to God about it; I then choose to not live under its control anymore and ask God to renew my mind and to feed me with the truth that will transform me.

If after reading this, you realise that like me, you have had negative attitudes to God's Word, then maybe you'd like to pray this prayer with me?

> Father God, thank You for Your Word. Thank You that it is living and active. It is the life-changing Word of Jesus. Please forgive me for every way I have both consciously and unconsciously responded to Your Word out of negative experiences. I give all of these to You. I do not want to be controlled by them any longer. I want my spirit to be transformed by the truth that Your Word is exciting and beautiful. Please work this through in my life by the power of Your Holy Spirit. In Jesus name, Amen.

From there, how can we develop the expectancy that God's Word will penetrate our innermost beings and change us into His image? That we will discover the keys to defeating the devil? That we will come to know God more and more fully? That we will be both comforted and empowered?

PRAYER AND THE HOLY SPIRIT

In his book, Paul Yonngi Cho, went on to say: "I pray to the Holy Spirit, 'O Holy Spirit open my eyes that I that I may see the truth of God in Thy Holy Word.' What a joy it is to read the Word after prayer."[3]

The end of this phrase is the key to discovering the transforming power of the Word of God. It was prayer that opened up the Bible to Cho. When we pray we are welcoming the Holy Spirit to come alongside us and reveal the truth of what we are reading to our spirits. As Jesus said,

"... the Counsellor, the Holy Spirit, whom the Father will send in my name, will teach you all things and will remind you of everything I have said to you."

(JOHN 14:26)

The Holy Spirit is the one who loves to make the love and purposes of Father God alive to us. He is the one through whom Jesus whispers His words of encouragement and challenge into our hearts. The Holy Spirit takes the love gifts of Jesus, our bridegroom and brings them to us, the bride, and then lovingly helps us to discover what they are and how to use them. Sometimes we can pray and talk about the Holy Spirit as if He is some kind of power tool. But He is a person, the third person of God and our counsellor, our friend.

WE HAVE BAPTISED IMAGINATIONS

The writer C.S. Lewis coined the phrase "baptised imaginations" to describe the fact that we have been given the mind of Christ. The fullness of our mind's power, logic, memories, intuitive understandings, and ability to empathise and imagine, are all redeemed and renewed when we trust in Christ. When the Holy Spirit speaks to us He uses our baptised imaginations as the notepad for His words.

A PERSONAL ENCOUNTER

Last week I was on a time of retreat. On the first night the retreat leader suggested prayerfully reading through a selection of verses. I asked the Lord to bring the right verse alive to me, nothing particularly grabbed me, then I came to Isaiah 55:1–11: *"Come, all you who are thirsty, come to the waters ... "*

That was it! I stopped at that word "thirsty". It was as if one finger was pointing to that verse and another to my heart. For so long I'd felt barren inside. Yes, I knew God loved me; I would sense His anointing as I taught and served Him, but my personal spiritual life was a dry ache. I was always busy, fitting lots of different things into my life, but then a deep pain of futility would hit me out of the blue. Now as I prayed, the Holy Spirit was bringing this to the surface.

As I reflected with God through this passage it was as if a holy spotlight shone into deep areas of my life. Things I'd pushed down and denied; coping strategies that I'd raised up in their place; unbelief in God's love that makes me avoid coming trustingly into His presence ...

The pattern of the whole retreat was set for me by that one word "thirsty" as enlightened by the Holy Spirit. At the end of the retreat there was a definite shift in my innermost being. Buried things were laid to rest, coping strategies dealt with, unbelief turned to belief that I am dearly loved by God.

So How Does it Happen?

Maybe after reading this you are feeling: That's all very well, but *how does it happen?*

Firstly, it's important to realise that there are no hard and fast methods, but simple ideas can help us to discover both God and ourselves through His Word. Our calling is to be a holy, radiant bride for God our bridegroom. As in any love match, God longs for us to know Him as He really is, to understand and enjoy Him, to work together with Him, in other words, to worship Him.

The Bible, the *whole* Bible, not just the familiar easy bits, is like God's autobiography, His invitation for us to discover Him. Through the Holy Spirit He gives us the "spectacles" we need to read beyond our human blur.

REFLECTION

One word that I have used often in this chapter is "reflect". This is the practice of holding before your consciousness the object of your thought.

Pardon?!!

Imagine a cow chewing the cud. Where we chew food quickly, swallow, and it's gone, a cow goes through a lengthy digestive process of chewing, digesting, chewing, digesting ... This is what we need to do when we reflect!

You read some verses. In reflection you then let your mind drift over what you have just read, turning it over in your thoughts, considering it from one angle, looking at it from another. You look "through it" at God, you shine it onto yourself; you note down anything that seems to strike you as significant. You talk to the Lord about that and take note of any illumination you seem to receive. This is reflection and it applies to all aspects of hearing God.

LED TO A PARTICULAR TEXT

God may want to speak to you through a particular text in a given moment. This is what we refer to as the *rhema* word of

God. It is when a verse takes on a direct, personal, "now" meaning to you. This was what happened to me with the word "thirsty" from the Isaiah passage. In that instance I was reflecting on all the suggestions waiting for one to hit the bulls eye. You will know this has happened by a feeling of "YES" inside as you read. Alternatively, you may be praying (or worrying!) about something and suddenly have a strong feeling that you should read a particular passage. You turn to it, reflect on it, and it becomes God's promise, or prayer strategy, or teaching point for you, or a way of confronting the enemy.

When this happens, reflect! Take time too to apply the questions that I have suggested further on.

Imaginative Meditation

The Bible is full of stories and picture language. One very illuminating way to hear God is to imaginatively put yourself into a story and see how God speaks to you through it.

For example, an exercise:
Read the story of Zacchaeus hiding in the tree (Luke 19:1–9). Conjure the scene of the story to your mind, the crowds, the heat, the urgency of Jesus' mission. Then put yourself in Zacchaeus' shoes. It may be that you literally imagine yourself in a tree, or it may be that you think of the kind of places you yourself hide in. What was happening in Zacchaeus' heart? Why had he climbed the tree? What was he afraid of? What did he long for?

Think of yourself with those same questions. Now "see"

Jesus coming and looking up, knowing you are there. What is the expression on His face? Hear Him calling your name. How does His voice sound? How do you feel when you hear your name called by Jesus? Think of what Jesus said to Zacchaeus that brought him down so quickly. Listen for what Jesus says to you. Don't dismiss any idea that comes, instead note it down and treasure it. Look at Zacchaeus' response; how can you respond to Jesus?

HAVE A REGULAR PATTERN OF READING THE BIBLE

This does *not* mean forcing ourselves to read a certain number of chapters at a certain time every day – for most of us, life pressures prevent that. But try to read regularly over as big an area as possible. I may read some Old Testament history and a New Testament letter on one day; another day I may focus on an Old Testament prophet and a New Testament gospel story. A third day may see me in the Psalms or Proverbs ... I may read a bit of something in the morning and another bit before I go to bed. I will continue in those particular books to their end and then move on to others. It may be that one day I've spent an hour, another only ten minutes! We are all different. Some of us need to be more systematic, but it is a fact that if we spend approximately fifteen minutes a day reading the Bible, we will cover it in a year. There are many "One-Year Bibles" nowadays which break the Old and New Testaments down into manageable daily readings. There are also a vast number of Bible reading aids. I use UCB's *Word for Today* which has a daily verse and thought which are very helpful to get me going in the mornings! It also, like many, has a year reading plan.

The important thing is not just that we read, but that we take in and feed on what we have read. It is not the reading that enables us to grow, but how it is ingested. Listen to how Jesus responded to the devil's temptations to satisfy what must have been a raging hunger.

"It is written: 'Man does not live on bread alone, but on every word that comes from the mouth of God.'"

(MATTHEW 4:4)

In this response Jesus was living out what He was saying. It was because He, throughout His life, constantly took time to read, reflect, take in, apply and worship God through His word, that when the moment of crisis came He had a well inside to draw on.

How Do We "Eat" God's Word?

Here are some simple questions we can have in mind as we approach any Bible passage.

First of all, remember that you are not sitting an exam! You are simply reaching out to the One who loves you so passionately. When I was first a Christian and upset because I couldn't hear any sermons, friends suggested imagining that I was sitting with a much loved friend and visualising Him pointing his finger at different words and phrases saying, "Look this means this, that means that ..." This helped me a great deal and of course, it is true! Maybe you would like to imagine that too?

What is the context?

This can be as in-depth as you want and have time for! It can be a simple matter of just reflecting on what was really going on in that particular story; maybe looking up cross-references to get a sense of the time and place or links to other events. Or you can go deeper and with study aids discover more of the background or the meaning of certain words and actions etc. This is very illuminating. I was enthralled recently to read about Jewish marriages in the context of the parable of the ten virgins and it really helped me understand that parable in a much deeper way.

How does God deal with His people – in this passage?

Look at the wider context. For example, if you are reading an Old Testament prophet and the passage is full of God's plan to bring judgement, it could give you rather a negative view of how He deals with His people! However, if you take the time to find out the background and then prayerfully reflect on it and what was really happening, it will give you an ongoing and deepening awareness of how God works with His people and what things bring Him joy or sorrow. Then you can apply it to yourself and our world.

How does the way the people relate to God and life teach me?

We can learn much from the way Bible characters related to God and to one another. Thousands of years separate us, but people's struggles, joys and griefs are everlastingly relevant. I was challenged by Daniel recently, how he handled an extremely stressful situation *"with wisdom and tact"* (Daniel 2:14). I realised that Daniel did not reserve his spirituality for the big prophetic moments, but revealed it in everyday responses to others. In fact, his powerful prophetic anointing sprang out of his faithfulness in making godly responses in his everyday life. This made me ask how important it is to me to always put God in the centre of the way I speak to people and react to circumstances?

What does it reveal to me about God's character and ways?

Paul prayed for the Ephesians that, " ... *the God of our Lord Jesus Christ, the glorious Father, may give you the Spirit of wisdom and revelation, so that you may know him better"* (Ephesians 1:17).

Paul and Jesus both prayed this. To know God better is one of the most important things we can ever do. Our picture of God can be so small. We know Him as Father, but not as Lord; We know Him as Saviour, but not as friend. We can ask as we read: "Is this another aspect of Him being Father, Friend, Lord?" The other day I was reflecting on the story of Jesus' response to the one leper who returned to thank Him. I saw that Jesus was grieved that the others did not return and He was so happy and affirming with the one who did. It was a revelation to realise the joy that it brings Jesus when we respond to Him with heartfelt thankfulness. I had often thought about Him as friend, but this was a new understanding of what *my* friendship means to *Him*.

What does it reveal to me about myself?

Jesus said, *"If ye continue in my word ... ye shall know the truth, and the truth shall make you free"* (John 8:31–32 KJV).

The Word of God is like a powerful torch shining on our

attitudes and actions. Jesus said that as we take in His word we truly become His disciples. We already belong to Him and nothing can alter that, but as we allow His word to change, heal, convict and comfort us, we become what we already are! His word sets us free from the old a little more every day.

When I was first a Christian I was in a state of emotional turmoil and hated the person I had become. I had accepted salvation and that had been a huge turnaround, but the pain was still there. One day some friends encouraged me to read this simple phrase from Isaiah 43:4: *"You are precious and honoured in my sight, and because I love you ..."*

I thought this just referred to Israel, but my friends explained that God's Word is eternally relevant and that He was saying those loving words to me right now. They told me to ask the Holy Spirit to enable me to see the truth about myself as I reflected on the words.

I felt so negative about myself, but I thought of those words and tried to see myself as someone "precious", "honoured", and "loved". A memory suddenly came of when a teacher had publicly discarded an Easter bonnet I'd made. Suddenly God put these words in my mind: "You created it in love because you knew in your heart how you wanted it to look. You chose the colours and you were excited as you imagined the finished result. When your teacher discarded it, you felt sad because even though it hadn't come out right it was still your creation. Child, I too created you in love, and chose the colours that would make you unique as a person. I grieved when the circumstances of your life crushed you, but child, unlike your teacher I will never discard you. Just as your creation was precious to you, so you are precious to Me, but where that was mocked and rejected, I tell you that you are loved and honoured and My perfect purposes for you will be fulfilled."

I was stunned by these prophetic words and at the sheer love of God, that He knew every detail of my life and could speak so lovingly into my pain by prophetically opening up a Bible verse. That was one of the milestones in my journey to finding healing and peace. On other occasions God has challenged me, maybe through one of the letters or stories, to look at ways I am judging or acting or responding to situations in fear rather than in trusting peace. He is daily seeking to make us more like His beloved Son. As we humbly reflect on our own lives in the light of what we are reading He will speak to us, never to condemn but always to set free.

What do I need to do?

When we read the Bible, we need to ask God, "Lord, how do You want me to apply this? Is there anything You want me to do?"

Listen to these words of James:

> *"Don't just listen to the word and so be deceived. Do what it says. If you don't, you are like someone who looks in a mirror and then forgets your own face! But when you look properly in God's Word and apply it constantly, knowing it will bring you true freedom, you will be blessed."*

(James 1:22–25 paraphrased).

BUT HOW CAN I APPLY IT?

An exercise

Have you come across the term "dialoguing with God"?

If not, it's very simple and essentially the same as what you do with people all the time:

- Read a passage from one of the New Testament letters.
- Reflect on some aspects of the above questions.
- Now say to the Holy Spirit, Lord, is there anything you want me to do?

Wait quietly, maybe lifting up in your heart anything that has earlier caught your attention in the words. That is often a sign that God wants to speak into a particular thing. It may be that you get an awareness that you need to pray in a certain way, to lay something down before the cross, to imaginatively release comfort over a hurting loved one, to wield the Word like a sword against a particular enemy stronghold. Or it may be that you need to change your attitude to someone or yourself. When God spoke to me prophetically through the "precious and honoured" verse, He showed me that I needed to choose to think from the position of that truth rather than from the old negatives. When the devil attacked, I had to recognise it as an attack and hold up that truth to push the attack away. I had to make my daily decisions on the basis of being someone precious and honoured rather than being someone pathetic.

PRACTICAL, BUT TO ME ESSENTIAL

One thing I have found invaluable is the practice of journaling. Sometimes I use a notepad and pen, especially when busy or travelling around. Mostly I use my computer. As I read a Bible passage I note any insights that come.

Then I express my response. I may write something like: "Lord, this Psalm says that You are full of loving kindness, those are lovely words Lord, but I don't quite know how to expect You to show me that kindness." Then as I pause and listen, I remember someone earlier smiling at me or sharing a bar of chocolate. So I write, "Oh Lord, was that You showing me Your kindness through that person? Thank You Lord ..." Then I write: "Lord, what else are You saying to me through this?" I realise that God also wants me to display His loving kindness as well as receive it. I write that awareness down together with the query, "How Lord?" It may be that I think of someone I haven't shown love to and I need to say sorry to God (and maybe to the person!). Or I think, "How I can bless someone that day ..."

Writing it down enables it to become real and helps you to see that you really are communicating with God. If you are concerned that you are just imagining things, check them against the Bible. It is tremendously uplifting to see afresh how God has spoken to you and how you have grown.

Notes

1. Paul Y. Cho, *Prayer, Key to Revival* (Word, 1984), p. 44.
2. Tracy Williamson, *The Voice of the Father* (Hodder & Stoughton, 1996), p. 37.
3. Paul Y. Cho, *Prayer, Key to Revival* (Word, 1984), p. 44.

CHAPTER 3

THE GOD OF CREATION AND EVERYDAY LIFE

"The heavens declare the glory of God;
the skies proclaim the work of his hands.
Day after day they pour forth speech;
night after night they display knowledge."
(PSALM 19:1–2)

My relationship with God was transformed about a year after becoming a Christian. I was frustrated because I could

51

not hear the sermons, but college friends pointed out that God taught the apostles by His Holy Spirit and He would do the same for me. It was exciting to start seeking Him in a fresh way. One day I read this verse from Psalm 19 and couldn't forget it. I thought, suppose it is true, that God speaks through creation. What would it mean?

Tremendously excited, I searched the Bible and to my amazement discovered that God indeed spoke to individuals through creation and even through the ordinary things of life. The psalmists, for example, repeatedly spoke about tuning into God through creation and receiving His strength and help:

> *"I lift up my eyes to the hills –*
> *where does my help come from?*
> *My help comes from the LORD,*
> *the Maker of heaven and earth.*
> *He will not let your foot slip –*
> *he who watches over you will not slumber . . . "*
>
> (PSALM 121:1–3)

This man who was obviously in trouble, deliberately looked away from his problems and sought God instead. As he gazed at the hills around him, the deeper understanding of the ability and desire of God to protect him broke through into his consciousness.

In a book, I read how Brother Lawrence, a fourteenth-century monk famous for "practising the presence of God", became a Christian as he gazed at the bare branches of a tree in winter. He was overwhelmed with the truth of God's regenerative love. His work in the monastery kitchens was transformed. His clumsiness had made it an unfulfilling trial, but he began to expect to meet with God through the simplest actions. Even picking up something from the floor became a means of communicating with God and worshipping Him.

I saw how Abram was spoken to personally and prophetically through creation. He was told by God to look at the stars after expressing his grief that he had no son. What a strange thing for God to say! But as Abram obeyed and first looked, then began counting the stars, God gave him a wonderful prophetic promise that he would have, not just one child, but so many that they would be innumerable (Genesis 15:2–4)!

I also had an encounter with God through the stars. I was depressed because I felt that my life had no meaning. One night, my pastor David suggested that I go outside and look at the stars. I hadn't a clue what he was thinking of, but later I did it. At first, all I could see was blackness. My dark feelings overflowed and I cried out to God. Suddenly, my eye was drawn to a tiny twinkling light, a star, then I saw thousands! The darkness had seemed all pervading, but now its power was fragmented by the beautiful light. I gazed from one to the other in wonder. It was as if I'd never seen them before, as if I'd only been aware of the darkness, ignoring the glory of the universe to which the darkness was just a backdrop.

I prayed silently, "Lord Jesus, what do You want to teach me?" It was amazing how alive the night sky now appeared. I felt very small in contrast to this revealed vastness of creation, but strangely I no longer found that frightening. Suddenly some scriptures came to mind:

"When I consider your heavens,
  the work of your fingers,
the moon and the stars,
  which you have set in place,
what is man that you are mindful of him,
  the son of man that you care for him?
You made him a little lower than the heavenly beings
  and crowned him with glory and honour."

(PSALM 8:3–5)

Through this, God spoke right into my heart, telling me that even as He had poured out His creative love into the universe, creating the stars with their individual stamp of beauty and setting each in its assigned place, in even greater measure He had done the same for me. I was not just a created "thing", but someone who was "just a little lower than the heavenly beings"! He knew and loved me and I too was in my assigned place where I could best shine out for Him.

From deep within I whispered, "Thank You Father, that in all Your immensity You made me and love me and I belong to You."

As David had known, God had spoken into my need. Not through human words of comfort, but through His own language – His creation – in this case, the stars.

An exercise

Take time to go outside with Jesus as company. Ask Him to open your mind to His presence and to speak to you by His Holy Spirit. Have a notebook to hand to record any insights.

You don't have to be in a particularly beautiful spot to

hear God through creation. Remember Brother Lawrence was just looking at a bare tree, Abram at the sky. Remember too that our pets, children and neighbours are just as much His creation as the trees and mountains!

Walk slowly or sit down and take in the scene around you. What can you see? What response does the scene evoke in you? Awe? Longing? Fear? Worship? Peace? Note down this immediate response.

If you are aware of any stresses or problems that are niggling at you, take this time to tell Jesus about them. Ask Him for His help and wisdom. Ask Him if there's any new perspective He wants to give you, if He wants to speak to you through anything you can see?

I was recently gazing abstractedly at a pond, but suddenly noticed the algae covering the water. As I prayed, God spoke to me about things in my life that were preventing me from being transparent.

Look around again, this time specifically focusing on the detail. See if your eye is drawn to anything in particular, a bud just opening, a cow chewing, a leaf moving in the breeze ... Say to God, "Lord, what do You want to show me through this?" Take note of any thoughts that come to you. Remember you have the mind of Christ and He will speak to you by giving you simple thoughts and ideas. Talk with Him about any insights, asking Him for wisdom to know how to receive them and be changed. Make a note of everything in your notebook.

GOD IS NOT COMPARTMENTALISED

We often feel that God is only interested in "spiritual

things" like our Bible study, but that understanding is far too limited. God is the God of life and He gives us that life to live to the full (John 10:10). As just seen, He speaks through creation. He is also interested and involved in the whole of our everyday life and anything can become a channel for Him to speak through. We see this principle operating throughout the entire Bible. For example, David heard the voice of God through his work as a shepherd; Jeremiah sensed God giving him a prophetic word as he watched a potter at work; Amos found that a bowl of ripe fruit carried a message from God, and Abram also received prophetic encouragement through grains of sand. In the New Testament, Jesus took this pattern to new heights. As He taught about the Kingdom of God, His words were so powerful that people were stunned by His authority, yet 80% of what He said was illustrated from everyday life: people farming their land, building houses, children wanting a snack, housewives looking for items, wine-making, bread-making ... On one occasion when His disciples queried this, Jesus quoted this searching passage from Isaiah 6:9–10:

> " 'You will be ever hearing but never understanding;
>   you will ever seeing but never perceiving.
> For this people's heart has become calloused;
>   they hardly hear with their ears,
>   and they have closed their eyes.
> Otherwise they might see with their eyes,
>   hear with their ears,
>   understand with their hearts
> and turn, and I would heal them.'

But blessed are your eyes because they see, and your ears because they hear."

(MATTHEW 13:13–16)

OPERATE ON TWO LEVELS

Jesus was expressing the fact that we have been created to operate on two levels. We can experience life with our natural senses and at the same time receive a higher communication from God. This however is not automatic. We have to make a choice to listen to God even in the midst of the most ordinary things. Jesus said that if we do this, then our hearts will be opened to God's love and we will be able to receive His healing. Conversely, if we do not do this, then our innermost beings will harden and we will become confined to a very narrow and restricted way of experiencing life. This is very challenging. We can't afford to lose this wonderful potential God has given us to know Him and be part of what He is doing. It is vital that we learn to "understand" and "perceive" what God is saying to us.

One of our prayer team, Lilian, once shared how God had spoken to her through a burn on her finger. It was a small burn but it blistered and kept weeping. Then one morning she found it had closed and almost disappeared. She was amazed how suddenly this had happened. God then told her that someone in the coming conference felt despairing about a heart wound that would not heal. He said that just as her finger had healed suddenly, He was working in that person's wound and they would find that suddenly it was healed and all the pain would be gone. In this situation, the process of tending a minor wound was transformed because Lilian had a heart to "understand" and "perceive" the higher level of what God wanted to say through it.

WE DON'T ALWAYS RECOGNISE WHEN IT HAPPENS

I once explained in a workshop how God speaks through these kinds of daily situations. I also emphasized that *all* Christians can hear God, but that often we don't believe it and therefore don't expect it to happen. A lady then shared excitedly how God had spoken to her that very day, but at the time she hadn't realised it. On her way to the workshop she had been climbing a steep hill. She saw a tandem bicycle ridden by a dad and his Downs Syndrome son. They were both pedalling furiously as they came up the hill, but after cresting it, the dad stopped pedalling and coasted down the other side. The son however, was still working as hard as possible.

This stayed in her mind and when I said that our noticing of something can be an indication that God wants to speak to us, she asked Him if this incident meant anything. She was amazed when the clear thought came back to her that she was like the Downs son, in that she was always striving to achieve when He simply wanted her to rest and receive His power and resources. She left that workshop full of joy. Firstly, because she knew this word was truly from God and it brought deep relief that she didn't have to strive anymore. Secondly, because she felt a new expectancy that anything and everything had the potential of being a channel for

God's voice, if only she took the time to listen and respond to His promptings.

How Can "Understanding and Perceiving" Come About?

There are five keys:

- Expectancy
- Awareness
- Holy comparison
- Conversing
- Interpretation and application

Expectancy

The woman who attended our workshop left with a new expectancy. Expectancy is a heart attitude of trust in what God says and in His character. The Bible says of Abram that after God spoke to him through the stars, "[he] *believed God, and it was credited to him as righteousness"* (Romans 4:3; also see Genesis 15:6). We think that righteousness means being as good as possible. This is not true. Righteousness means believing in God and believing that what He says and does is true. From that belief, God's power is released in us to make us more and more like His Son and to do His works. Jesus said repeatedly that all who believed in Him would do the things He was doing and even greater things (John 14:12). He said His sheep could hear His voice (John 10:27) and that He calls us His friends on the basis of the fact that He communicates the Father's heart to us (John 15:15). Our focus so often is our sense of worthlessness, which

God has already dealt with on the cross. Expectancy means changing this negative self focus to a true focus on Him.

Awareness

How do we really know that God is speaking? While we can truly say that anything *can* become a channel for His voice, not everything *will* be. God is not an indiscriminate chatter-box! He always speaks with a purpose.

The key to discerning that God is genuinely speaking through something is *awareness*. The dictionary defines aware-ness as "having knowledge or perception of a situation". In a spiritual sense this means an inner sense of knowing some-thing is significant. Your thoughts seem to go in a certain direction; you look at something and can't stop thinking about it; a certain phrase keeps going through your mind, or you become very conscious of the presence of God.

This awareness can occur in two ways. Firstly, it can be sudden, without any pre-effort on your part, as if the Holy Spirit has broken into your thoughts and drawn your attention to something. I believe this happened with Jesus as He sat by the well in Samaria (John 4). He was thirsty and the well's proximity caused His thoughts to focus on that thirst and His need for the water that would relieve it. He saw the woman approaching and was suddenly moved by the Spirit into an awareness of *her* deep inner thirst and the fact that *He* was the living water to relieve it. Jesus was not trying to deliberately tune into God for a prophetic word, He was just resting by the well! But because He always practised awareness, He recognised when the Holy Spirit broke into His thoughts to draw His attention to the well and the woman.

Secondly, awareness can and must also be a deliberate act of becoming still in our hearts and seeking to tune into God. This awareness is the heart realisation that God is with us. It is not so much that something bursts unannounced into our minds, but that we consciously lift up our minds to Him and invite Him to come in. We see this, for example one day when Jesus exhorts the disciples not to worry:

> " ... *do not worry about your life, what you will eat or drink; or about your body, what you will wear. Is not life more important than food, and the body more important than clothes?* **Look** *at the birds of the air; they do not sow or reap or store away in barns, and yet your heavenly Father feeds them. Are you not much more valuable than they? ... And why do you worry about clothes?* **See** *how the lilies of the field grow ... "*
>
> (MATTHEW 6:25–28 emphasis added)

Jesus wanted His friends to become aware of the Lord through their senses, taking in the things around them and expecting God to speak and minister into their spirits. The Greek meaning of the words "look" and "see" are much fuller than the English meaning. It means a deliberate looking, smelling, touching, listening, all our senses focusing on something, in this case the birds and flowers and then saying to God "Lord, what do You want to say to me through this?" This leads us on to the next key:

Holy comparison

A normal earthly "thing" becomes a channel of God's voice to us as we engage in "holy comparison". This means looking at it in its own context, reflecting on how it enables us to see and worship the Lord more fully and then, as He leads, comparing it with ourselves or God's character and ways. In the above example from Matthew 6, Jesus looks at the fact that God feeds the birds and comments, *"Are you not much more valuable than they?"* Our greater value, as God's beloved children, is the holy comparison here. We look at the beauty of creation, then understand that we are so much more valuable in God's eyes. In another example in Matthew 7 Jesus encourages His friends to ask God boldly for what they need. Here the illustration is taken from an everyday situation, children asking for food. The holy comparison is between our parent's responses and God's and realising the greatness of God's Father love for His children:

> *"If you, then, though you are evil, know how to give good gifts to your children,* **how much more** *will your Father in heaven give good gifts to those who ask Him!"*
>
> (MATTHEW 7:11 emphasis added)

Conversing with Him

We converse with one another all the time and we need to do the same with God. God will draw our attention to something, but that will never be the full revelation. Through talking with Him, asking questions, listening, asking for more understanding and listening again, we enter into what God wants to tell us.

I am deaf and so never hear first time what someone is saying. I ask them, "Did you say … ?" and then they tell me again. It may take quite a few goes before I understand what they are telling me. This is what we need to do with God,

because in a spiritual sense we are all partially deaf. We get a
hint of something and continue talking it through with Him
to get more insight.

Examples

One time I was ironing. I'd had an argument with a friend.
I knew I'd hurt her and was upset that I'd let this happen,
yet again. I tried to pray, but felt too tensed up. Suddenly I
found myself thinking specifically about the process of
ironing my shirt – the heat I needed to use, and the way I
moved the iron to best effect. I thought, why am I thinking
like this? Ironing is automatic! Then the Lord spoke into
my heart, saying, "When you iron, you see in your mind's
eye how you want your garment to look – perfect! Just as
you use the right amount of heat and steam to bring that
perfection about in your shirt, so I see you as perfect
already because of Jesus, and I know what 'heat' and
'steam' to use in your life to make that perfection real." I
was astonished and overwhelmed. To think that God
would speak to me in such a tender way when I was in
such a bad mood was staggering. I talked with Him, saying
sorry for my part in the argument and asking for help to
forgive my friend too. I finished that ironing with much
more enthusiasm!

A lady at a workshop could not see my face as I was
teaching because the overhead projector was in the way. She
felt irritated and in the meditation time couldn't get it out of
her mind. She asked the Lord if He wanted to speak to her
and as she listened, became aware that just as something
was stopping her from seeing my face, so there were things
that were blocking her from seeing *His* face. She was

shocked and asked Him what they were. Certain things came to mind and she talked with Him about them and asked His forgiveness. At the end of this conversation she felt a real peace that God had touched and released her. An incredible thing then happened as she returned to the room. I'd just decided to remove the overhead projector. She sat, looked up at me and could see my face with nothing in the way! She felt such a joy that God had given her this sign of His forgiveness.

Interpretation and application

Hearing God, even conversing with Him for more insight, can never be the end of the story. We also need to know how to apply what we have heard. In Acts we see how a word from God was given for Paul, but initially his fellow disciples responded to it out of fear rather than really hearing what God wanted:

> *"... a prophet named Agabus came ... he took Paul's belt, tied his own hands and feet with it and said, 'The Holy Spirit says, "In this way the Jews of Jerusalem will bind the owner of this belt and will hand him over to the Gentiles."' When we heard this, we and the people there pleaded with Paul not to go up to Jerusalem. Then Paul answered, 'Why are you weeping and breaking my heart? I am ready not only to be bound, but also to die in Jerusalem for the name of the Lord Jesus.'"*
>
> (ACTS 21:10–13)

The prophecy was accurate, but the disciples' interpretation and application wasn't. They saw it as a warning to keep Paul away from Jerusalem, whereas God was speaking in order to prepare Paul for what was ahead, and through that inner preparation to be able to reach out with God's love and power even to his attackers.

We need to keep reflecting and conversing with God to understand how to apply what He gives us. In a concert once, I saw a bouquet of flowers. I presumed God wanted to encourage someone that they were beautiful like the flowers, but then I noticed that some were dying. I asked God for wisdom. A scripture came to mind:

> *"All men are like grass,*
>   *and all their glory is like the flowers of the field;*
> *the grass withers and the flowers fall,*
>   *but the word of the Lord stands for ever."*
>
> (1 PETER 1:24–25)

God told me someone was building a huge business to get rich, but they had left God out. He said that if they didn't make room for Him, they would die, even in the midst of their prosperity. I was so shocked as this was very different from my initial response to the bouquet! I prayed again that God would enable me to know His heart. I sensed His yearning love for the person and believe that His love was communicated as I shared the word. I heard later that a prominent atheist businessman had gone forward for prayer to become a Christian!

An exercise

Have a notebook to hand. Thank Jesus that He is with you and has given you His mind and Holy Spirit. Place any worries into His hands and ask Him to speak to you and help you to draw closer to Him.

Bearing the above five keys in mind, try the following:

1. Sit in a room that is familiar to you. Look around slowly as if seeing it for the first time. Notice things like how organised or messy it is. How light is it? Are the curtains open or closed? Are there things in it that obviously display your character or is it quite impersonal? As you look, ask God to speak to you, both to draw your heart up to Him and to speak into your life and needs. Are there curtains of fear or shame shutting out the light of His love in your life? Are you putting on an impersonal front and keeping the "real you" safely tidied away? Talk to Him about any thoughts or ideas that come to your mind as you look around.

2. Get on with a familiar job or activity, e.g., cleaning, filing, building etc., but ask God to speak to you through it as He did with Jeremiah as he watched the potter (Jeremiah 18:1–6). Are there any parallels between what you are doing and what God does or wants to do? Is there anything He wants to speak into your life to challenge you in any way? Take note of any insights and talk about them with Him asking Him for more wisdom and understanding.

Once, as I washed up, I realised that a cup needs washing just the same as a greasy tin. Similarly, we all need washing in the precious blood of Jesus, whether we feel we've sinned much or not! Just as our kitchenware is made sparkling clean, in even greater measure, we are made sparklingly pure and holy. I shared this insight with a friend who was feeling very worthless. None of my consoling words had had any effect until then, but this "went in" and in moments she became joyful and free!

CHAPTER 4

HEARING GOD THROUGH HIS CHILDREN

*"The tongue that brings healing is a tree of life,
but a deceitful tongue crushes the spirit."*
(PROVERBS 15:4)

As a child I was crippled emotionally by words that stripped away my self-esteem. Even though I went on to higher education, I saw myself as a failure. I'd heard so often that I was unlovable and mentally deficient that I'd come to believe it. A school friend once joked: "I think Tracy is a good name for you because it is meaningless!" It was only a passing comment, but it struck home in my heart. I forgot about the conversation and her words, but they remained like an arrow in my heart together with all the other negatives. I felt like a shell with nothing inside but pain and the fear of being exposed for what I was.

But God loved me. God sought me out through that student who invited me into her room and told me that I needed to know God as Father. I was overwhelmed. It seemed incredible that God would bring *me*, of all people, to her mind. She had a dynamic personality, but as I looked at her, I saw warmth and kindness and I heard it too in the inflexion of her voice. Something responded from within me. A hope was born, a different kind of arrow went into my heart and it bore fruit. It made me seek out God and want to know more about Him.

God was speaking to me through His child Ruth. He was putting His words in her heart for me and giving her His love-expression of those words. All of this had a tremendous impact on my soul. After I became a Christian, He continued to speak to me through His children. Christians told me that God loved me. A young couple in my church invited me to be with them for family times like Christmas and holidays. They talked, prayed and listened to me. They also asked me to do things that no one had ever trusted me to do before.

In all these ways God was speaking to me. He was telling me that I was loved, that I had worth and could give as well as receive. Sometimes the contacts were not as direct, but God was still speaking powerfully through His children. I would find myself in tears in the middle of a sermon. A phrase would catch me and something would open up inside. This was God speaking through the pastor's words into an area of hurt in my life. Once I wept as I watched a little girl climb happily onto her daddy's lap and saw the tender way he hugged her. That man was completely unconscious of the fact that God was using him to speak to me of the tenderness of His love. He was just being his normal self, but I can still feel the power of God's gentle words through him today.

When I was twenty-one I met Marilyn Baker. I was depressed because my career plans had collapsed. She was an established Gospel singer, I was still a new Christian with no idea what I should do with my life. But we became good friends. One day she said, "I really believe that God may use you in full-time ministry sometime."

With those words a door of hope was opened up within me. Suddenly I knew that I had value as a person, that there was something I could contribute. On the one hand it seemed an incredibly presumptuous thought. How could I even think about God using *me?* I was so weak! On the other hand, I experienced a deep sense of rightness. It was as if Marilyn's words had confirmed a desire that I didn't even know I had!

It was just four months later that God opened up the way for me to join Marilyn in her full-time ministry and I've been with her ever since. At the time, Marilyn didn't know that she was speaking prophetically. In her mind she was just chatting, but God had put that thought in her heart and spoke through those casual words into my spirit. In this case, although the words still had a strong healing effect, they were also God's words of guidance and direction to bring me into the centre of the plans He had for me.

WE ARE CHRIST'S AMBASSADORS

I have shared some of my personal story here in order to emphasize the incredible responsibility God has given us to impact those around us with His words of transforming love. Whether we consciously realise it or not, we are His witnesses and we carry and display His presence and character with us wherever we go. As Paul says,

> "... he has committed to us the message of reconciliation. We are therefore Christ's ambassadors, as though God were making his appeal through us."
>
> (2 CORINTHIANS 5:19–20)

God longs for people to be reconciled with Him. This does not just mean initially when we are saved, but for the whole of our lives. God wants the minds, spirits, souls and bodies of each one of us to be brought into an ever-deepening healing and intimacy with Him. This comes about as we fulfil our ambassadorial role, consciously giving and receiving God's love, allowing our whole lives to be channels for Him to speak through. The apostle John claims that the degree to which God's love will be known and experienced depends on the degree to which we give it to one another. This is why the words and actions of love that I received and witnessed after becoming a Christian had such an impact on me. God's love was being made complete in my life though the way His children gave it to me.

How Does God Speak to Us Through Others?

If we look at the life of Jesus we see how He communicated the love of His Father God to everyone He met. He preached, and people were challenged by His sermons; He engaged them in conversations, listening to what they said as well as speaking to them; He literally went out of His way to respond to peoples' needs; He told stories that had an instant non-religious rapport; He sat children on His knees, physically hugged people, and empathised with the emotional isolation of their illnesses by touching the affected areas; He used relational names like "daughter" or "son" and affirmed peoples' faith; He rebuked people and was not afraid to be straight with them; He listened to God through the Holy Spirit and received appropriate spiritual gifts like the ability to see into men's hearts, prophesy and minister healing and deliverance.

Jesus said that He could do or say nothing other than what He saw His Father doing. All of the above were ways in which Jesus spoke God's love into peoples' lives. It wasn't simply that this was just the kind of man He was. He was actively communicating through word and deed the transforming love of the Father to all who had ears to listen. You can sense His grief at His disciples' failure to understand this:

> *"Don't you know me, Philip, even after I have been among you such a long time? Anyone who has seen me has seen the Father. How can you say, 'Show us the Father'? Don't you believe that I am in the Father, and that the Father is in me? The words I*

say to you are not just my own. Rather, it is the Father, living in me, who is doing his work."

(JOHN 14:9–10)

Remember, God has called us to be His ambassadors. Where God spoke and acted through Jesus' words and actions, so He now speaks and acts through ours. It is vital that we have ears to hear what He may tell us through someone else. It is also vital that we step out in the power God has given us to speak His words of transforming love and do His acts of grace and compassion.

An exercise

Take some time to be quiet with Jesus. Have your journal to hand. Ask the Holy Spirit to still your heart, inspire and speak to you.

Read Mark 1:40–42.

- Imagine the leper who came to Jesus seeking to be healed. It says that he begged Jesus on his knees. What does this show you about his emotional condition? Remember that his leprosy made kneeling costly and painful. What does that reveal about the state of his heart? Think of his plea: *"If you are willing, you can make me clean."* Does that tell you anything about his level of expectancy?

- Think about yourself. Is there any area in your life or in the life of someone you love where you long for Jesus to do something? How far have you gone in expressing your longing to Jesus? Are you honest in your expression of faith? How do you think He will respond?

- Look at the way Jesus does respond to the leper. How does He speak to him? What does His voice sound like? It says Jesus was "filled with compassion". How do you see that in this story? What kind of messages from the Father would you say Jesus was giving the leper through His response?

- How do you think Jesus responds to you? Think of a time when you have been listened to, when someone has shown they understand, when you have been smiled at or hugged and helped with your need. Have you realised this was Father God speaking to you? Have you received it from Him and taken it in? If not, tell Him you want to now. Thank Him for speaking through someone's words and actions and tell Him you want to recognise every time He does speak to you in this way.

- Think of ways in which you respond to people. Do you take time to pray and hear God's heart for those around you? Are you aware of your words and actions and the effect you may have on someone? Think of a particular person. Ask God for wisdom to know how to bring His love to them through your words and actions. Take note of anything that comes to mind and then actively step out in what He has given you.

The Wonder of the Spiritual Gifts

Earlier, I said about Jesus that He listened to God through the Holy Spirit and received appropriate spiritual gifts. The spiritual gifts are one of the key ways that God equips us to speak His words of love to one another. All the gifts are given to all of His children in order to communicate His love in a dynamically powerful and life-changing way, so that Christians are edified and built up in the truth and love of God. As Paul says,

> "... *everyone who prophesies speaks to men for their strengthening, encouragement and comfort.*"
>
> (1 CORINTHIANS 14:3)

Prophetic words come in many different formats. It may be direct words and phrases as if God is speaking them Himself; it may be parallels taken from everyday life and creation; it may be pictures, dreams and visions; it may be through a tongue and its interpretation; it may be through a prophetically inspired sermon or song, or it may be some symbolic gesture or action. Whatever the format, the words are coming from the heart of God in order to minister His comfort, encouragement or challenge and direction. Whether for an individual or a group like a church fellowship, the gifts are always given to draw people close to God and enable them to be transformed into His likeness. We need to listen to God in order to know what He wants to say to others and also to listen to what He is saying through others to us. We need wisdom to understand not only how to move in the gifts, but also, to recognise when and what God is saying to us.

NOT ALL PROPHECIES ARE FROM GOD

Jesus was without sin and was therefore the greatest of prophets. There was no "self" in anything He said and His words cut straight into peoples' hearts with the power of God.

Like Jesus, we are fully dependent on the Holy Spirit to function in the gifts. They are the most powerful way of impacting people with the love of God, but we need great humility and wisdom in the way we use them. There will always be an element of "self" in our prophecies and this is where we need to recognise that we are fallible and can often have hidden motives like the desire to be noticed, or to have a role, or to influence people.

If one way has worked once we tend to think, "I've sussed it!" On one occasion Marilyn and I prayed with a lady crippled by arthritis. We sensed that she was wounded emotionally and she told us her daughter had been raped by the babysitter. We prayed she would be healed of the grief and guilt she had carried so long and at the end she was wonderfully at peace. The next morning we had fantastic news. She'd woken up and for the first time in twenty years was able to dress herself without pain!

I was so thrilled with what God had done through this word of knowledge that I made it a method! I told everyone with arthritis that they had some deep inner wound or guilt that needed healing first. I was pigeonholing them with my certainty that this was God. It took someone becoming quite upset to realise what I was doing and stop!

How Do We Respond to Prophetic Words?

Don't treat prophets as God!
Because prophets are speaking as from God we can attribute a greater authority to them than is wise. Prophetic words are not meant to control and direct our lives but

to confirm what we already sense from God in our own spirits. We should never relinquish our responsibility to hear God for ourselves. I heard a story of the devastating results that can occur when we base everything on a prophet's words:

A young woman went forward to receive some prayer ministry. To her amazement, the counsellor began to pinpoint some things in her life that no one knew about. This man is a true prophet, she thought, and listened to him with close attention.

At some point she mentioned that she was engaged and would soon be getting married. At this, he said, "I believe God is saying that this is not the right man for you. If you are obedient to the Lord and give this man up, then in a year's time you will marry the man that God has chosen to be your husband."

At great cost and heartbreak she broke off the engagement. Each time the sadness threatened to overwhelm her, she tried to comfort herself that in just a few months she would marry the right man. As the months went by she started looking at every man with new eyes. A year came and went, no man, no husband. Two years, nothing. Devastated and broken she is now receiving counselling.

The prophet in this story was on the right track for as long as he brought the words of knowledge which were truly from God. Maybe when he saw her awe and incredulity as each detail was revealed, he was tempted to bring what he thought was a word of direction from the Lord. His mistake was in abusing God's powerful gift by using it to control. Her mistake was to base such a costly life decision on another's words, even though it went against the grain of all her heart was saying.

But don't be put off! If we listen with humble hearts of wisdom, discernment and faith, we *will* receive treasures of healing, affirmation and guidance through others.

A lady came to Marilyn and me for prayer, but because I could not hear her, I was not sure of her need. As I prayed quietly, a picture came to my mind of an under-stair's cupboard. The door was shut but I could sense there was a great deal of rubbish behind it. Then God said, "She fears that there is a lot of rubbish there and won't look inside. She is too ashamed and is not trusting in My forgiveness, but see what *is* behind that door." In my picture I saw the door then being opened and instead of a pile of rubbish, it was all empty and clean.

I shared this with her and discovered that she had been feeling very guilty about an accumulation of sins. She couldn't believe God could forgive her. She was overcome by the picture and knew that God was telling her she was completely forgiven.

It is awesome that God speaks through us like this. I was only able to help this lady because of this powerful word from the Lord. On my own I could not even hear her, but even if I could, I still would not have been able to work up just the right thing to say. Only the Lord knew just what she needed to hear in that moment. In His mercy He gave it to me to share with her and she was set free from all her guilt.

As we saw with Jesus, ministering God's heart is always far more than merely speaking words. It will be conveyed through the tone of our voice, the expression in our eyes and the touch of our hands, just as much as by the prophetic word itself. When I received that picture I had already been praying in my heart for the lady. I was affirming in prayer that she was precious to God and was asking Him to bless and comfort her in her distress. I asked, "Lord, how do You want to love and help her right now?" It was then that the picture and its interpretation came to me. When I shared it with her I used smiles, touch and gentleness of tone to convey the joy of the Lord's forgiveness. As Paul said, our very lives are like letters written by God (2 Corinthians 3:2). Prophecy and the other spiritual gifts can never just be like something we read out like an email, but our very beings expressing the heart of God.

But of course, this lady had to choose to believe what God was saying to her at that time. Paul said,

> *"Not all the Israelites accepted the good news. For Isaiah says, 'Lord, who has believed our message?' Consequently, faith comes from hearing the message, and the message is heard through the word of Christ."*
>
> (ROMANS 10:16–17)

When the word of Christ is given, whether it is a prophetic word, a sermon, a hug, or a prayer, it has no power to change and heal unless it is heard with faith and accepted as truth. There is always that dynamic between what God gives and how we choose to receive it.

After I shared that picture, the lady had three choices: She could smile sadly, shake her head and say, "That's lovely, but you don't know me ...": she could beam and thank me, but leave with her heart still full of condemnation; or she could smile, thank me and take into her heart the truth of what it meant for her, and so receive God's comfort, strength and encouragement. Wonderfully, she chose the third option and was healed and set free.

TURNING AWAY FROM UNBELIEF

It is a tragic fact that in our present society we believe more in the destructive power of negative thinking than in the liberating truth of God's love. Bitterness and cynicism are the gods of our age. The fear of rejection is worn like the national costume! Often we totally lack any sense of self-awareness and responsibility. We love to put the onus for our lack of spiritual progress onto others or even onto God, rather than dare to let God show us our own heart condition. We say, "God does lovely things for others but not for me"; or "Christians are always rejecting me. No one ever understands or listens to me" etc. If you say to such a person, "You are really precious to God. He loves you as His son/daughter; He cherishes you and has wonderful plans for you . . . ", invariably, they will smile cynically, shake their heads and dismiss it. They prefer to put their faith in what they perceive as the negative "proof" – their treatment by others. While it is true that amongst Christians there is often a tragic lack of love and sensitivity, and much rejection, cruelty and abuse under the cover of respectability, it is also true that many in the church are trying their hardest to reach out with God's affirmation and love. Yet, if someone hugs us we often stiffen and push them away, or think inwardly, "You may hug me, but it doesn't mean anything, so and so just ignored me so that's the real truth!"

God's heart is broken when we wound one another with rejecting or bullying words and actions. He feels our pain and weeps with our tears. He loves those who are lonely and rejected. It was primarily peoples' hardness of heart to one another that caused Jesus to speak His most scathing words. When we act in this way it is as if we are wounding and crucifying Him all over again. But in His love, He took it all with Him to the cross to free and heal us. Jesus was rejected in the most extreme way, by His friends, family, people He had loved and helped, even by His Father God. He endured it so that the stranglehold of rejection could be broken and healed in our lives. He poured out His forgiving love and gave us His power to forgive as He forgave.

A prayer

If after reading this you know that you have failed to hear God's words of love and affirmation through His children and have instead dwelt on the negatives and allowed them to shape your faith and control your ability to receive, then maybe you'd like to pray this prayer with me?

> Father God, thank You that You love me. Thank You that You heal and transform me. Thank You for every time You use Your children to speak Your words of love to me. Please forgive me that I have pushed You away by not believing these words. Please forgive me for focusing on negative experiences rather than forgiving and letting them go. Lord I want to have a new focus – You and the wonderful ways in which You give Your love to me. Please give me eyes to see, ears to hear and a heart to receive every time You

speak to me through Your children. Please fill me with Your love that You may speak Your words of love through me into the lives of others. In Jesus' name. Amen.

CONCLUSION

A MEDITATION

The three friends had no idea where Jesus was taking them. They'd seen Him spending time with women, beggars and filthy children; they'd watched with glee as He'd stripped rich hypocrites bare. They expected Him to surprise them. But now, what was He doing? They'd been climbing this mountain for so long and all for what? There were no beggars up here in this barren wasteland!

Suddenly He stopped. "Wait here," He said, and before they had time to think, He had moved away.

It was then, before their eyes that He changed. An incredible radiance came over Him. Majestic, awesome, there were no words to describe His glory. Other, godlike figures came and stood alongside Him, it was beyond imagining. As Peter stumbled out something incoherent about shelters, they heard it, that deep stilling voice from Heaven:

"This is my Son, whom I love; with him I am well pleased. Listen to him!"

The very earth vibrated with the power of the words and terrified, they fell down. They couldn't move until He touched them. They opened their eyes and saw that the Jesus they knew was back. Relieved and shaken, the awesome details soon began to blur. But those words they could not forget: *"This is my Son, whom I love; with him I am well pleased. Listen to him!"* (Matthew 17:1–13).

THE MOST CRUCIAL THING

On that momentous day, those disciples learnt the most crucial thing that a Christian can ever learn. There is nothing more important, than for us to know and listen to God.

Listening to God is the basis of all effective service to Him. We cannot reach out with God's compassion and divine power without knowing Him and His ways. We cannot know Him and His ways without listening to Him and communicating with Him.

In this book I've tried to share out of my personal experiences of listening to God. Repeatedly, I fall into a rut and lose all desire for Him. But every time I seek Him, I find His eagerness to love and speak to me far outweighs mine for Him! He never gives up and I am awed and humbled by such love.

"This is my Son, whom I love ... Listen to him!"

It is my prayer that this book has helped you respond, not just in a passing moment, but with your life, "Yes, beloved Lord, I'm listening."

About the Author

Tracy Williamson was born in 1964 in North East London. At the age of two she became ill with encephalitis, which left her deaf and partially sighted with coordination difficulties. The hearing loss was not discovered until Tracy was twelve, which meant that she was often thought to be a slow learner. When Tracy was seven her father died of cancer. Soon afterwards a new father came into the family. He was a violent tempered man and Tracy suffered verbal and physical abuse from him throughout her teen years.

These childhood traumas had a huge negative impact on Tracy's life and she became very introverted and depressed. Despite that and her deafness, she pushed forward in her academic achievements, becoming a wide reader and gaining GCSE and A-levels, excelling particularly in English. When she was eighteen she was offered a place at what is now Hertfordshire University to take a teaching degree in the hope of becoming a teacher of the deaf.

Tracy's first year at college was fraught as she came to realize that she couldn't simply leave her past behind. Also her deafness made the teaching of children too stressful.

After a long period of anguished soul searching Tracy made the decision to give up her dream of teaching the deaf and transferred to a BA Degree in English Literature and Education. This whole process made her desperate for real answers and help in her life and after many conversations with Christian students, she became a Christian in June 1983. Tracy then went on to complete her degree, gaining a 2.1 (Hons.) in June 1985.

MINISTRY

In that same year, prior to forging a career with the visually impaired, Tracy met with blind singer/songwriter Marilyn Baker and a deep bond of friendship formed between them. Marilyn's assistant left in January 1986 and Marilyn asked Tracy to help her out temporarily. It soon became apparent however, that God was calling Tracy to the ministry and she gave up her proposed course to become Marilyn's personal assistant in April 1986. She is still in this ministry today.

TRACY'S ROLE

Initially Tracy's main role was to be a practical support and administrative assistant to Marilyn. However, it soon became clear that God had anointed Tracy with gifts of communication. Beginning with sharing her testimony in concerts, Tracy then began to receive prophetic words for individuals and churches. As her prophetic gifting developed, Tracy realised how few people expected God to speak to them personally. This led to her volunteering to do a workshop on listening to God at a conference led by Jennifer Rees-Larcombe in

1993. The workshop was a great success and ultimately led to the publication of her first book *The Voice of the Father* which was published by Hodder & Stoughton in 1996.

Since then Tracy has written a number of articles promoting Marilyn's albums for various Christian publications. She has also written for Scripture Union's Bible reading notes series *Closer to God*, including a series on "The Father Heart of God" in 2001 and on the book of 2 Timothy in 2004. Tracy now regularly teaches at workshops, church weekends and conferences that she and Marilyn lead together. Some of the areas she teaches on are: prophetic prayer and ministry; listening to God; intimacy with God; the Father heart of God; breaking out of loneliness; overcoming fear and anxiety, and becoming the true body of Christ.

We hope you enjoyed reading this New Wine book.
For details of other New Wine books
and a range of 2,000 titles from other
Spirit-filled publishers visit our website:
www.newwineministries.co.uk